A GIFT FOR:

FROM:

Published by Hallmark Gift Books,
a division of Hallmark Cards, Inc.,
Kansas City, MO 64141
Visit us on the Web at Hallmark.com.

Editorial Director: Delia Berrigan
Art Director: Chris Opheim
Designer: Mark Voss Design
Production Designer: Dan Horton
Contributing Writers: Jeannie Hund, Catherine Hollyer, Katherine Stano, Ellen Brenneman, Renee Daniels, Suzanne Berry, Melvina Young, Cheryl Hawkinson, Linda Elrod, Mary Miro, Alarie Tennille, Eva Allen, Teresa Leggard, Stacey Donovan, Linda Staten, Tom Shay-Zapien, Diana Manning, Kimberly Schworm Acosta, Melissa Woo, Anna Wenner, Carolyn Hoppe

ISBN: 978-1-63059-700-9
1BOK1413

Made in China
0618

THROUGH THE STORM

WISHING YOU A BREAK IN THE CLOUDS

I wish I could make this go away for you.

The questions, the worries, the frustrations . . .

it all must be such a heavy load to bear.

But despite how tough this is, I want you to know

I believe you're even tougher.

This is not the first time life's thrown you a curve.

You've already shown time and again

what a strong, determined person you are.

I have no doubt that your inner strength

will see you through this, too.

I can't make this go away,

but I can assure you that you're the

same wonderful person I've always known—

and nothing can change that.

Something like this takes courage and patience

and probably more energy than you have some days.

But I hope it helps to remember that I'm on your side.

I want you to know that I'm here for you,

that you can tell me how you really are—

on your good days, your bad,

and all the ones in between.

You don't have to sugarcoat anything.

Nope. Not for me.

I may not know what you're going through,

but I do know that I want to stand by you

to listen, understand, encourage you, and cheer you on.

To give you a hug when you want one

or a laugh when you need one.

To picture you, when you're out there

living life your way again.

So just think of me

as a little support group of one,

reminding you every single day

what an amazing person you are.

It takes courage to claim joy

in this world.

It takes a powerful heart,

determined mind,

and beautiful spirit . . . just like yours.

I just hate it when crappy stuff happens to good people.
I'm so sorry that you're hurting right now and that this is so hard.
I could say all the usual stuff about how strong you are
and how you can cope with this. But when stuff like this happens,
even a strong person can feel sad, tired, and overwhelmed.

That's where friends come in.

To keep reminding you about the strength you've got inside

and to lend you some when you're running low.

I've got extra from the last time you lent me some.

Need it back?

Just ask.

I'm here for you.

You don't have to be strong all the time.

It's OK to let down, to lean on others,

to just be.

You don't have to do anything
but remember that you're loved.

For all the times you've been there to listen,

now it's my turn to be there for you.

You've calmed my fears so many times—

let me be the one you rely on now.

Let me remind you how strong

and resourceful you are.

If you can't trust yourself, trust me—

I'm here for you through this.

You always find ways

to be encouraging and supportive.

Now it's my turn to be

the one you can lean on,

the one you can count on,

the one you can be real with.

That's the role you've always filled for me . . .

Let me be here for you now.

You are your own hero, and hope is your sidekick.

It seems like a person should only

have to handle a certain amount

of stress at one time.

But it looks to me like the needle

on your personal stress-meter

is at an all-time high.

This, of course, is completely unfair.

You don't deserve any of it.

If I had some magic words

to make everything better,

this would be a good time to say them.

Instead, I'll just have to say

I'm thinking about you

and I care about you very much.

And I really believe in you.

You're pretty amazing.

And impressive. And strong. And brave.

But mostly amazing.

Life would be so much easier

if there were some sort of master plan—

if we could anticipate the highs and lows

and prepare accordingly.

But that's not how things work.

I know you're riding one of those lows right now,

so I'm wishing you the strength and resilience

to deal with life's troubles,

so that you can ride high on life's triumphs.

I hope peace and comfort

find their way to you,

wherever you may be on your journey.

When life gets hard,

when it seems that everything

is working against you,

and even the simplest thing

you try to do gets complicated,

just remember:

You are loved.

When life gets ordinary,

when the day-to-day routine

hardens into a boring rut,

and nothing you do seems important,

or even worthwhile—

When the world seems to hold more gray clouds

than silver linings,

just remember:

You are loved.

Through the good times

and the bad times,

nothing can stand in the way

of the special, powerful love

that's meant for you alone.

Wishing you more of everything you need to get through this.

Your way of handling things

has been impressive.

Other people might fall apart,

but you forge ahead,

with faith in yourself.

That takes a lot of courage.

But you have a spirit

that can't be held down . . .

an optimism that inspires

everyone around you.

And as someone who cares about you,

I want you to know that

I admire you tremendously . . .

that you're in my thoughts

and prayers.

I'm also sending you

wishes for good days ahead,

for comfort and for joy,

and, of course, for love.

Because you deserve it all.

Remember to seek the joy in every day.

Name it, claim it, celebrate it—

however small or life-changing

that joy may be.

It is intended just for you.

A real victory isn't
in sailing through life,
having everything come easy,
but in getting knocked off course,
taking stock, making changes,
and launching out again.

A real champion isn't always
the one who reaches the summit
on the first or second try,
but the one who has the patience
and the wisdom
to set a new course
when unexpected storms come along.

Real strength doesn't mean

always winning,

but instead,

giving it your all.

And sometimes it means

taking heart from the support
of others who believe in you and care.

I see you do all of these things.

And I want you to know

you are a hero in my eyes.

I wish I could make

the world right again,

the sun bright again,

your heart light again.

What I can do is send you

a world full of love

and all the hugs you can handle.

It's amazing to me . . .

you've been through so much lately.

Still, you remain steady and calm.

I don't know how you do that.

But, I so admire it.

You live in the moment

and find beauty in everything.

No wonder I love being around you

and appreciate you like crazy.

I'm sorry for the tough stuff

you have to deal with.

Through it all,

please remember

how much you're loved,

how much I care,

and how wonderful—

truly wonderful—you are.

Be filled with love.

Be surrounded by light.

Be peaceful. Be radiant. Be broken, too.

Be you.

One of the worst things

about dealing with something painful

is feeling isolated and alone.

That's why I want you to know

that I'm here for you

when you need

a listening ear

or a loving hug.

I'll be thinking of you every day

and cheering you on,

knowing that

you'll face each day

with courage and hope,

because that's the kind of person

you are.

Cozy in your heart.

Warm deep down in your soul.

And very, very loved.

Hope that's how you're feeling today.

Sometimes, when the going gets hard,

all you can do is take life day by day . . .

relying on the wisdom

your heart has learned

through the years

and relying on the friends you've made—

friends like me.

With all my heart,

I want to help you see

all the beauty life holds for you.

So please: Lean on me.

And together,

we'll get through this, day by day.

In times when questions outnumber answers

and uncertainty is all that's certain,

know without a doubt that

you're being held closely in the hearts

of so many who love you.

People might say,

"You've got this!"

Which can make you feel like,

"Why don't I have this?"

And you might question

why you can't handle what's happening,

even though people say you can.

But you know what?

This is hard.

And if you're not completely, totally

on top of everything,

that is more than OK.

You have nothing to prove to anyone.

Just take it one day at a time,

and know that those of us

who love you are here,

no matter what.

Some days it's a little easier

to see the light

coming through the clouds

and feel a bit of peace.

I hope this is one of those days.

Everyone has ideas about how

you should manage this chaos.

The thing is, there's no right way to do this,

and there's no wrong way to feel.

So whatever you decide to do,

I hope it gives your heart the peace it so deeply deserves,

and know I'll support you.

It seems like such a cruel trick—
the way the world goes on about its business
while you handle all of this.
You've been through so much already,

and others have no idea of the burden you carry.
But I hope you know there are those of us
who have not forgotten and
hold you close in our thoughts.

Whether you're having a good day,

a not-so-good day,

or something in between,

please remember that every day

you're loved because you're you.

Sometimes we're stuck living in the Unknown.

Will things get better?

Will things get worse?

Will things get worse and then better?

The Unknown doesn't say.

As long as you're stuck in the Unknown,

know you've got me.

Little pockets of peace
tucked between warm moments
and the knowledge that you are loved.
That's what you're wished today and every day.

Everyone who loves you
is right there with you.
You may already know that,
but what you may not know
is the reason.
Never think it's only because
you're going through this rough time.
No, it's much, much bigger than that.
We're with you because we need you,
because you're one of us,
because whatever happens to you,
good or bad,
happens to us, too.
We're with you
night and day, all the way . . .
just as we know you'd be there for us.

Wisdom flows through your words.

Goodness radiates from your smile.

Strength defines your every step.

And I am so honored to know you.

This can feel like a roller coaster.

And not the fun kind.

One minute you think you're OK,

and then WHAM.

The bottom drops out

from under you.

I wish that you weren't going through this

and that life were easier somehow.

But if you need a hand to hold

or someone beside you

through the ups and downs . . .

I'm here, and I care.

HOPE and HUGS

are coming your way.

Hope you can feel how much

you're loved.

I know your heart hurts.

I wish I could make it better

with a kiss and a Band-Aid,

and maybe an ice-cream cone.

But broken hearts

don't work like that.

They need time

and lots and lots of love.

So, I'll give you all the love I have,

all the hugs you want . . .

and probably some ice cream

just in case.

It's OK to feel whatever you're feeling.

You don't have to smile.

You don't have to pretend.

You just have to take care of yourself

and remember that you'll always be important

and you'll always be cared about.

I've seen you stand up

to some pretty trying times—
recover from some defeating days.
I've watched you lift others
with your courageous kindness—
spread joy with your powerful heart.
That is why today I want you
to give some time, some kindness, and love
to your very precious, very tender,
one-of-a-kind self.

Whatever inspires a feeling of well-being,

whatever connects you to those you love,

whatever warms every little corner of your world . . .

that's what you're wished today.

Right now,

it might feel hard to do the simplest of things.

Sometimes,

it might feel difficult to even move.

So please,

let those of us who love you

meet you there.

Let us sit with you

and help you make sense

of the chaos.

Let us reassure you

that there will be breaks in the clouds

when the sun will shine through

and you will feel its warmth.

When it feels like life's given you

more than you can handle,

remember this:

Life's also given you

caring people in your world

to help you carry the load.

Count me among them.

You are a person of courage and strength,

and nothing can take that away.

No circumstance that comes into your life

can alter who you really are.

You are a person of kindness and warmth

with uncounted gifts yet to give.

No matter how stormy the world is around you,

your spirit shines through.

I wish for you

fresh air to breathe,

some time to just be,

and comfort,

like a soft shawl

around your shoulders.

If anybody ever deserved

a lot of support,

it would be you.

You're the one

who's always there

when people need you . . .

and it's time to let others

do some "being there" for a change.

Because you mean a lot.

I hope you know that it's OK

to just take it day by day

or even minute by minute if you need to.

Let the plan be to not have a plan.

Just do whatever you've got to do

to get through.

Cloudy with a 100 percent chance of rain.

That's probably how it feels

to go through something so tough.

But one of these days,

the sun's going to peek through

and bring back a little bit of light and color.

And until it does,

I'm going to be right here . . .

standing beside you,

holding an umbrella,

and watching for the first sign

of a rainbow.

If you enjoyed this book
or it has touched your life in some way,
we'd love to hear from you.

Please write a review at Hallmark.com,
e-mail us at booknotes@hallmark.com,
or send your comments to:

Hallmark Book Feedback
P.O. Box 419034
Mail Drop 100
Kansas City, MO 64141